1

The coast of Australia was very long. These were all salt water.

3

There were saltwater lakes and rivers for fish and birds.

5

The ocean had many fish. Fish was good food.

The water had plants called sea plants. These are called seaweed. Sea plants were eaten by some of the First People.

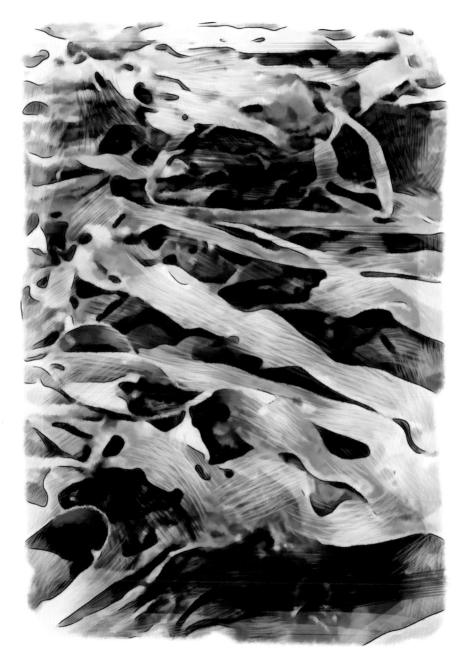

9

The coast had big animals in the water. The whales came close to the shore.

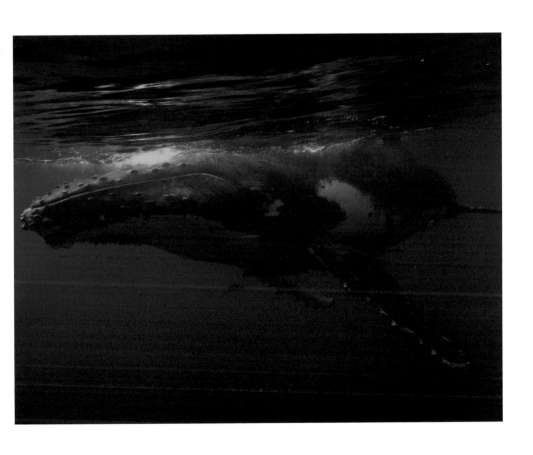

The sand hills had plants to eat.

13

The First People lived along the coast.

15

There are great hills of shells.
The hills were called middens.

16

17

Birds, eels and fish were in the lakes. These were caught with nets and spears.

On the beaches there were shell fish. This was called a pipi.

20

There were many types of plants near the salt water.

23

Word bank

shell   seaweed

spears   animals

caught   whales

middens   shore

plants

coast

Australia

saltwater

lakes

rivers

birds

ocean

food